Where are these people standing?

They are inside the Statue of Liberty.
Millions of people visit this huge **statue**
each year.

The Statue of Liberty is a famous
American **symbol**. The statue stands
for **liberty** and **opportunity**.

The statue is of a proud woman. She wears robes and a crown.

In one hand, she holds a torch high.
She holds a **tablet** in the other hand.

On the tablet is the date July 4, 1776. That is the day the United States of America was born.

Americans were once ruled by the British king. They fought a war for their freedom. France helped the United States win the war.

France and the United States became friends. Many French people wanted to honor the United States with a gift.

A French artist named Frédéric Auguste Bartholdi had an idea. He said that everything in America was big! He would build a big statue for Americans.

11

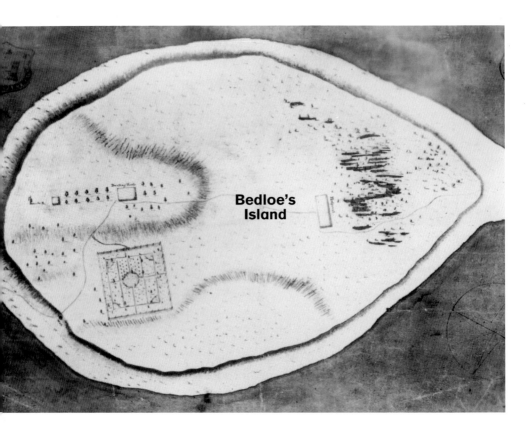

Bedloe's
Island

Bartholdi found the perfect spot for the statue. It was Bedloe's Island in the **harbor** of New York City.

Workers began building the statue in Paris in 1875.

They hammered copper sheets into the right shapes.

Later, workers nailed the copper sheets to a huge iron frame.

Bartholdi and his crew finished the
statue in 1884. Then it was taken
apart and sent to the United States.

There the statue was put together for the second time. It was finally ready in 1886.

Americans held a big celebration on
October 28, 1886. Thousands of people
came to see the proud lady of liberty.

The Statue of Liberty became a famous symbol of the United States.

She proudly stands tall for America's freedom.

Her shining torch glows in the harbor.
The torch stands for America sending
the light of freedom into the world.

In the late 1800s, the Statue of Liberty stood for something else. She became an important symbol for **immigrants**.

People came to the United States from
other countries. Many immigrants
arrived on ships in New York Harbor.

The Statue of Liberty welcomed millions of immigrants. She was a symbol of their hope for a better life.

By the 1980s, the statue needed lots of fixing up. She got a shiny new torch. Her copper skin was cleaned. Bolts were tightened.

The repairs were celebrated in 1986, on the statue's 100th birthday.

The Statue of Liberty is known all over the world as a great American symbol. She will always stand tall for freedom.

Facts about
the Statue of Liberty

The Statue of Liberty stands 305 feet tall.

The statue's pointer finger is eight feet long.

Each eye is as wide as a doorway.

Bartholdi used his mother's face as a model for the statue's face.

When the statue was taken apart to be sent to the United States, its pieces were packed into 214 crates.

The statue's full name is *Liberty Enlightening the World*.

At the statue's feet are broken chains. These stand for America breaking free from British rule.

A Warm Welcome

In 1883, an American named Emma Lazarus wrote a poem about the Statue of Liberty. It is about how the statue welcomes people seeking a safer, better life in the United States. Part of the poem is posted on a sign at the statue's base. It reads:

Emma Lazarus

Give me your tired, your poor,
Your huddled masses yearning to breathe free,
The wretched refuse of your teeming shore.
Send these, the homeless, tempest-tost to me,
I lift my lamp beside the golden door!

29

More about the Statue of Liberty

Books

Drummond, Allan. *Liberty!* New York: Frances Foster Books, 2002.

Rebman, Renee C. *Life on Ellis Island.* San Diego: Lucent Books, 2000.

Ross, Alice and Kent. *The Copper Lady.* Minneapolis: Carolrhoda Books, Inc., 1997.

Whitman, Sylvia. *Immigrant Children.* Minneapolis: Carolrhoda Books, Inc., 2000.

Woodruff, Elvira. *The Memory Coat.* New York: Scholastic Press, 1999.

Websites

The Statue of Liberty National Monument
http://www.nps.gov/stli/

The Ellis Island Official Website
http://www.ellisisland.org/

Visiting the Statue of Liberty

Visitors to the Statue of Liberty in New York City ride a boat to get to Liberty Island. The boat also stops at Ellis Island. Many immigrants landed on this island before entering the United States.

The Statue of Liberty

by Jill Braithwaite

Lerner Publications • Minneapolis

To Lauren and Kendra, two proud and free ladies

Text copyright © 2003 by Lerner Publishing Group, Inc.

This book is available in two editions:
Library binding by Lerner Publications Company, a division of Lerner Publishing Group, Inc.
Soft cover by First Avenue Editions, an imprint of Lerner Publishing Group, Inc.
241 First Avenue North
Minneapolis, MN 55401 USA

For reading levels and more information, look up this title at www.lernerbooks.com.

Words in **bold type** are explained in a glossary on page 31.

Library of Congress Cataloging-in-Publication Data

Braithwaite, Jill.
    The Statue of Liberty / by Jill Braithwaite.
        p.   cm. − (Pull ahead books)
    Summary: Provides an introduction to the Statue of
Liberty, including the history of its creation and its
importance as a national symbol.
        ISBN-13: 978−0−8225−3802−8 (lib. bdg. : alk. paper)
        ISBN-10: 0−8225−3802−4 (lib. bdg. : alk. paper)
        ISBN-13: 978−0−8225−3756−4 (pbk. : alk. paper)
        ISBN-10: 0−8225−3756−7 (pbk. : alk. paper)
        1. Statue of Liberty (New York, N.Y.)−Juvenile literature.
2. New York (N.Y.)−Buildings, structures, etc.−Juvenile
literature. [1. Statue of Liberty (New York, N.Y.) 2. National
monuments. 3. New York (N.Y.)−Buildings, structures, etc.]
I. Title. II. Series.
F128.64.L6 B73 2003
974.7'1−dc21   2002011836

Manufactured in the United States of America
6-42873-3163-9/12/2016